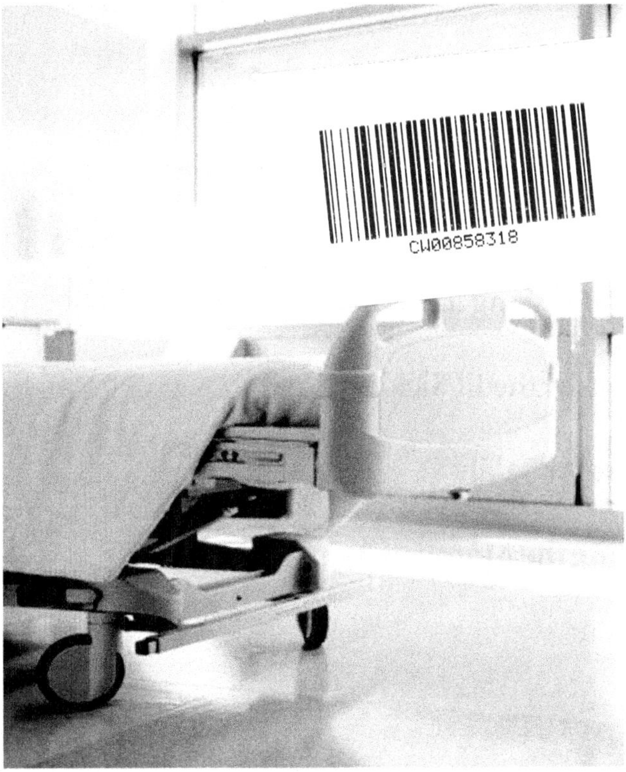

THE TEST OF ILLNESS

[A Great Test From Allah Ta'ala]

Fisabilillah Organization Authenticate Ulama's Organization

Published By: The Way of Islam, 6 Cave Street, Preston, Lancashire, PR1 4SP

CONTENTS

INTRODUCTION

Ill Health - A Great Test From Allāh

**"Do men imagine that they will be left (at ease)
because they say, 'We believe,' and will not be tested?
And certainly We tried those before them,
and Allāh will make manifest those who are true
and He will make manifest the liars."**

Qur'ān, al-`Ankabūt, 29:2-3

Life in this world is a great test from Allāh ﷻ, a test to determine the truthful ones from the liars. Allāh ﷻ tests his servants; in particular those who claim to believe and follow the Truth, by placing them in varying circumstances in order to see how they respond. Will they turn to him in humility and faith or turn away through pride and disbelief?

Allāh ﷻ has declared,
**"And be patient and persevering:
For Allāh is with those who patiently persevere."**

Qur'ān, al-Anfāl, 8:46

Abū Hurayrah ؓ narrated that the Prophet ﷺ said, 'If Allāh wishes good for somebody, He afflicts him with trials.' al-Bukhari

As believers it is our responsibility to remember that we are not in this world merely to enjoy ourselves, but rather to strive for the betterment of our eternal abode, the Ākhirah (Hereafter). Our primary concern should not be how comfortable our lives are in this world, but rather what we have prepared for ourselves in the hereafter.

The Prophet ﷺ beautifully put the life of this world into perspective when he said, 'This world is the prison of the believer and the paradise of the disbeliever.' Muslim

Just as prisoners expect themselves to go through adverse times, away from the freedom and enjoyment they may experience when free; as believers we should expect the same in these short lives of ours. Similarly, just as a prisoner will look forward to the day they are set free to enjoy the freedom they were deprived of, we, as believers, should also look forward to the day we will, hopefully by the grace of Allah, be set free to enjoy the pleasures of Jannah (paradise).

This doesn't mean that we cannot worry and strive for the betterment of our lives in this world, but the important point is that worry regarding anything of this world shouldn't become our greatest concern.

Ibn `Umar ﷺ related that the Prophet ﷺ would often supplicate, "(O Allāh!) Do not make the world the greatest of our worries..." at-Tirmidhī

Our Anxieties in Comparison to Others

Whatever anxieties we may experience, whether through ill health, physical or psychological pain, being diagnosed with a terminal illness, the death of someone close to our hearts, etc, it often becomes easier for us to bear if the tribulations faced by others are considered. By looking at those who live around us, those in third-world and war-torn countries, those who have lost not one but numerous members of their families, it creates a feeling that the deep pain we feel is not felt by us alone, but rather it is something shared, felt and understood by many others.

We may go a step further and look at the pain and suffering that those before us went through. Allāh ﷻ states in the Qur'ān,

"Or do you think that you shall enter Heaven without (facing)
They were affected by suffering and adversity,
and were so shaken that even the Messenger
and the believers who were with him cried:
'When is the help of Allāh (to come)!'
Verily, the help of Allāh is (always) near!"

Qur'ān, al-Baqarah, 2:214

One can only imagine the extent of the torment that the people of the past experienced - often only because of declaring their belief in one God - that even the Messenger ﷺ among them, who would be the most patient and persevering, would be forced to call for Allah's ﷻ help.

Khabbab ibn al-Aratt ؓ narrated, "We (the companions) complained to the Messenger of Allāh ﷺ (of the persecution inflicted on us by the non-believers) whilst he was sitting in the shade of the Ka`bah, resting on his cloak. We asked him to seek help (from Allāh) and pray to Allāh for us.
He replied, 'Among the nations before you a (believing) man would be put in a ditch that was dug for him and a saw would be put on his head and he would be cut into two pieces; yet that (torture) would not make him give up his religion. (An example of another person is that) his body would be scoured with iron combs that would remove the flesh from the bones; yet even this would not be able to make him abandon his religion.'" al-Bukharī

III Health - A Blessing in Disguise

Ibn `Abbās ⬥ reported that he heard the Rasūl of Allāh ⬥ say, 'There are two blessings in regards to which most people are in a loss, (they are) good health and free time.'

al-Bukhārī

Health is a great favour from Allāh ⬥, a favour we often remain ungrateful of and unmindful towards until it is taken away. The Prophet himself asked for good health and taught his followers to do the same.

`Abbās ⬥, the uncle of the Prophet ⬥, narrated that he asked the Prophet ⬥ to teach him what to ask for from Allāh ⬥. The Prophet ⬥ replied, 'Ask for good health from Allāh.'

at-Tirmidhī

Ibn `Abbās ⬥ narrated that the Prophet ⬥ said, 'Value five (favours of Allāh ⬥), before (the coming of) five: your youth before your old age, your good-health before your illness, your wealth before your poverty, your free time before your becoming occupied, and your life before death.'

al-Ḥākim

Although health is a great ni'mah (favour), this doesn't mean illness and disease cannot also be a favour from Allāh ⬥. Indeed every occasion for a believer can be an opportunity to attain closeness to the Almighty. This is achieved when at the time of ease one expresses 'Shukr' (gratitude) and at the time of distress one expresses 'Ṣabr' (patience).

Suhaib ⬥ reported that the Prophet ⬥ said, "How marvellous is the state of the believer? Everything that happens to him is good, and this does not apply to anyone except the believer. If something good befalls him and he is grateful for it, it is good for him. If something bad befalls him, and he bears it with patience, then too it is good for him."

Muslim

The Purpose of Life

It may also be become easier to deal with problems we may experience in this life by realizing the true purpose of our lives.

Allāh ﷻ states in the Qur'an,
"I have only created Jinns and men, that they may worship Me."
al-Qur'ān, az-Zāriyāt 51:56

Therefore, whatever trials or afflictions we may have to go through; it should only be of concern if it prevents us from fulfilling the true purpose of our creation, which is to worship Allāh ﷻ alone. It is often due to our forgetting the true purpose of our creation and life in this world that we take things related to this world more seriously than we should, whereas a firm believer upon realising the true purpose of his/her life will not be bothered to a greater extent unless something comes between him/her and worshipping Allah ﷻ. Such a firm believer will remember Allāh ﷻ at all times, in prosperity and adversity.

Ibn `Abbās رضي الله عنه reported that the Prophet ﷺ said, 'The first to be called to enter paradise are the ones who praise Allāh at times of prosperity and adversity.'
aṭ-Ṭabrānī

Elevation Due to Sickness

As has been mentioned earlier, Allah ﷻ has promised that He is with those who patiently persevere. In addition to that Allāh ﷻ has also promised relief from the suffering.

"Verily, with every difficulty there is relief."
Quran Ash-Sharh 94-6

However one should understand that this delivery from suffering can be in two forms. The first and most hoped for is actual cure or physical release from the pain. The second is not usually recognized by people, and this is that a more comfortable and relieving afterlife is being prepared for us because of the pain that we are bearing.

Abū Hurayrah ﵁ narrated that he heard the Messenger of Allāh ﷺ saying, "No fatigue, illness, sorrow, sadness, hurt or distress befalls a Muslim, even if it were a prick he receives from a thorn, but Allāh expiates some of his sins for that.' al-Bukhari

Once the Prophet ﷺ entered the home of Umm al-Musayyab ﵂ and asked as to why she was shivering, She said, "It is fever and may it not be blessed by Allah." To this the Prophet replied, "Do not curse fever, for it expiates the sin of the children of Ādam just as a furnace removes the scum of iron. Muslim

Sa'd ibn Abi Waqqas ﵁ narrated that he asked the Prophet ﷺ as to who was the most severely tested people. The Prophet ﷺ replied, 'The Prophets then their like and then their like (in terms of piety). A man is tested in accordance to (the strength of) his faith. If his faith is very strong his assessment is severe and if his faith is weak then his assessment is in accordance to it. A servant will continually be tested until it will leave him walking on the earth free from sin (i.e. his patience will be a source of expiation for his sins). al-Ḥākim

Anas ﵁ narrated that he heard the Prophet ﷺ say, "Indeed the greatest rewards are accompanied by the greatest trials; as when Allāh loves a nation, He tests them. Whoever accepts the trial willingly, earns His pleasure; and whoever resents it, earns His wrath.' at-Tirmidhī

Thus, from the numerous Aḥādīth mentioned, we learn that illness or any other calamity which may befall someone does not necessarily mean Allāh ﷻ is unhappy with them or that he is punishing them. Frequently it is the complete opposite where Allāh ﷻ wishes to elevates someone's rank and therefore places them in such a situation through which that rank may be attained.

Unfortunately, it is common to see someone who is suffering complain of their illness or misfortune resorting to statements such as "why me?" or "couldn't it happen to anyone else?" not realising that Allāh ﷻ has given them a chance to gain a great reward for their patience or a chance to escape the severe punishment of the Hereafter by experiencing a little discomfort in this world. On the other hand, by uttering such statements or harbouring such thoughts, one will not only lose this opportunity to reap a vast reward, but may even earn the wrath of Allah ﷻ. May Allāh ﷻ save us all. Āmīn.

Concessions for the Ill/Sick

If conditions are met, Islām recognizes and provides concessions for those experiencing difficulties such as ill health. These include concessions in how to attain purity, how to offer prayer, what to do about fasting, etc. It is vital that these concessions, along with the conditions required to qualify for them, are studied and remembered; so that one may take a concession when allowed, so as to avoid excessive and unnecessary exertion; and also so that a concession is not taken unlawfully.

These concessions and when they are applicable will now be broken down into separate sections and discussed under their own headings.

Rulings Regarding Purity

To be in the state of purity from both, Aḥdāth (minor state of impurity - which makes one require Wuḍū') and Janābah (major state of impurity - which makes one require Ghusl) is a prerequisite for many acts of worship. It is often the case that for one reason or another, an individual may not be able to perform Wuḍū or Ghusl at all, or that one may have a problem with remaining in the state of purity for long enough to offer a certain act of worship. Such cases will warrant the application of a concession.

Concessions on Istinjā'

A paralysed person, or one who is so sick that he cannot use water for Istinjā', or someone who is instructed that using water for Istinjā' may cause him harm or delay recovery, should use toilet paper or its like, through which cleanliness can be attained. If one cannot even manage to do this, then one must still perform Ṣalāh even if it means Istinjā' is not performed.

For those who cannot remain in the state of purity due to the continual or frequent occurrence of any Wuḍū'-breaking act or that one may have a problem with remaining in the state of purity for long enough to offer a certain act of worship, the regulations of a Ma`dhūr (lit. excused) may apply.

A Ma`dhūr is a person who is in the above situation, this can take form in many different ways, e.g. constant nose bleed, bleeding from a wound or the dripping of urine continuously, etc. (Note: if the wound can be bandaged then a different rule will apply, this will be explained in bandages/dressings.)

If one is in such a situation for the period of one complete Farḍ Ṣalāh in which one does not find sufficient time wherein Wuḍū' can be performed and Ṣalāh can be performed without the reoccurrence of the problem, then one has become a Ma`dhūr.

Once a person becomes a Ma`dhūr, it is not a condition that the problem should remain with such unrelenting consistency. As long as the problem occurs even once in each subsequent prayer time then one will still be classed as a Ma`dhūr for that prayer time. However, if one complete prayer time passes without the occurrence of the problem then one will no longer be a Ma`dhūr in status and as such, the concessions will also not be applicable. For a person to become a Ma`dhūr again after that one will have to face those conditions again that brought about the Ma`dhūr status in the first place.

The concession granted to a Ma`dhūr is that they will perform Wuḍū' only once in each Ṣalāh period, with which they may carry out all the various prayers and acts of worship in that time with that Wuḍū' in tact. During this time, the occurrence of the problem which caused one to become a Ma`dhūr will no longer render the Wuḍū' invalid. However, the occurrence of any of the other aḥdāth will cause Wuḍū' to be nullified and necessitate its renewal. Also, when the time of the prayer ends, Wuḍū' will automatically be nullified, and it will be necessary to renew the Wuḍū' for the next Ṣalāh.

Bandages/Dressings

If a bandage/dressing can be opened with ease and the skin underneath can be washed, such that it will not cause pain or delay the healing time, then it is necessary to open them (the bandage/dressing) and wash the skin during wuḍū and ghusl. Otherwise, if opening the bandage is harmful or may delay recovery; Masḥ (passing a wet hand over the bandaged area) may be performed. If the dressing (e.g. a plaster) on a wound can be taken off and replaced after the area has been washed, this must be done.

If a wound is open, and washing that area may be harmful, then to perform Masḥ upon the area is permissible, even if there is no bandage worn.

If Masḥ is also harmful, then neither washing nor Masḥ is necessary and that area can be omitted during Wuḍū'/Ghusl.

Even though one may be bleeding, with a bandage on one may perform Ṣalāh as long as the blood does not seep through or around the bandage. If blood, pus or other bodily matter does seep out, then the bandage/dressing should be changed.

If during Wuḍū' or Ghusl, Masḥ was performed upon a bandage or dressing which was then removed due to the wound healing, it is necessary to wash that area as Masḥ is no longer a concession.

Tayammum

Tayammum is a concession given to both those who do not have access to water to perform Wuḍū' or Ghusl, or those who may have water but are unable to use it because it may cause them to become ill or delay recovery from illness.

Tayammum is a symbolic method of attaining purity which can be performed off all clean earthen materials, e.g. sand, soil, rocks, marble, etc.

Tayammum has three Farā'Iḍ (necessary components):

1. Intention - This must be made such that one is performing tayammum, this does not have to be verbal.
2. Wiping the face - The palms of the hands are gently struck on the sand or soil, and then (after shaking off any dirt) used to wipe the entire face (as in Wuḍū').
3. Wiping the arms - Repeat the above but wiping the two arms instead of the face. (Also as in Wuḍū' the elbows should be included in what is wiped).

Tayammum can be performed as a substitute for Wuḍū and/or Ghusl. In any case it is performed in the same way.

Once tayammum has been performed, any act of worship can be performed with that purity. Unlike the Ma`dhūr, there is no time limit in the validity of Tayammum. Tayammum is rendered invalid by those things which render Wuḍū' invalid (or Ghusl if it was done in its place). The only other thing to invalidate Tayammum is the instance of water becoming available to use again.

Doubts Relating to Cleanliness

Abu Hurayrah ﷺ narrates that the Messenger of Allah ﷺ said, "Indeed, Allah has overlooked for my nation the misgivings/thoughts that occur in their hearts..." al-Bukhārī and Muslim

In regards to cleanliness and even acts of worship, the overriding principle is that certainty is not annulled by doubt.

This means that if an act of cleanliness (e.g. wuḍū') is definitely performed then the act will not be broken by a doubted action. Despite this, it is still better to perform wuḍū' again if one has the time. The following is an example of this:

If one clearly remembers performing wuḍū' but cannot truthfully remember if it was then broken or not, the ruling is that wuḍū' is retained. If, however, one then remembers that it was broken then wuḍū' and any subsequent acts of worship that required wuḍū' will have to be repeated. This is why it is better to repeat the wuḍū' if possible.

The same principle applies to ghusl, however, due to much more potential for invalid acts of worship, if one has any doubt in such an incidence it is much better to perform ghusl again to be safe.

Concessions for Ṣalāh

Ṣalāh is an essential part of faith and is farḍ (obligatory) on every sane, mature Muslim. However women in the state of menstruation or post-natal bleeding are exempted from its performance. (Please refer to Fīsabīlillāh book: "Key to Purity" for detailed rulings on this topic.)

In the state of illness, Ṣalāh remains farḍ, although some concessions may apply:

Sitting or Lying Down During Prayers

To stand and pray Ṣalāh is farḍ. To sit and pray a farḍ Ṣalāh without a valid excuse will render the prayer void. However, one is allowed to perform Ṣalāh sitting down if one is too sick or weak to perform the Ṣalāh standing, or if standing causes great pain, or even if it may increase the injury/illness. One may also perform Ṣalāh sitting if one is able to stand but cannot go into rukū` or sajdah. Someone who can stand for a little while should begin their prayers standing and thereafter sit and continue when necessary.

If a person does not have the strength to make rukū` or sajdah, then the rukū` and sajdah should be made by ishārah (gesture), i.e. by bowing the head slightly for rukū` and slightly more for sajdah. It is incorrect to raise something (e.g. a pillow or board) towards the head.

If a person cannot perform Ṣalāh sitting, then they should perform it lying down, i.e. lie down on the back with the legs facing the Qiblah. The knees should be raised slightly when doing this. If the knees cannot be raised then one can stretch one's legs towards the Qiblah. The head should rest at a higher level with a pillow under it. Rukū` and sajdah will be done by gesture.

One may also lie down on the right side facing the Qiblah or even on the left side if necessary. It is preferable to lie on the right side if one has a choice.

If someone cannot move any part of their body but their head, then ishārah of the head will suffice during Ṣalāh. If one cannot even move their head then Ṣalāh should be delayed - Ishārah of the eyes is not valid. (If, immediately after being in such a state, a person were to pass away, then the missed prayers would be forgiven, and Fidyah would not be necessary. This will be explained further on).

Note: As long as one remains conscious then Ṣalāh remains an obligation.

Note: If a sick person's bedding or clothes are najis (impure) and changing them would cause great inconvenience, then Ṣalāh may be performed despite this.

Note: The above may also apply to a woman who is heavily in pregnancy.

Falling Unconscious or Being Too Weak to Pray

If a person remains unconscious for less than a full day and night, he/she must perform all the missed Ṣalāh.

If one remains unconscious for a full day and night or more, then one need not perform the Ṣalāh one has missed. One is exempted from performing them. And as there is no Qaḍā' (making up of missed prayers), there is no institution of Fidyah.

If a person is conscious but has no strength even to move the head as ishārah, then he/she should not perform the Ṣalāh immediately but should wait until regaining their strength. When one regains strength, Qaḍā' will have to be performed for the missed Ṣalāh, even if the condition lasted for more than a day and night (unlike the case of someone being unconscious).

If someone is genuinely unable to perform Qāḍā' of the missed prayers due to illness or weakness and recovery from this condition is not expected, they will have to give Fidyah to the poor for each Ṣalāh missed, if they can afford it.

Jumu`ah

Jumu`ah Ṣalāh is necessary upon all mature, sane males although the sick and weak are exempt from this.

Women, the sick and the weak will perform Ẓuhr Ṣalāh, however, its obligation would be fulfilled if they did join the Jumu`ah prayer.

If someone does want to perform the Jumu`ah Ṣalāh then the congregation has to consist of at least four people (three besides the Imām) and the Khuṭbah (sermon) must be delivered before the Ṣalāh.

Illness During the Month of Ramaḍān

Ṣawm (fasting) in the month of Ramaḍān is Farḍ on every sane, mature Muslim. Although women will not fast during menstruation and post-natal bleeding, unlike with Ṣalāh, they are required to make up the missed fasts on a later date.

Someone who begins a farḍ fast and thereafter, because of weakness or illness cannot continue with the fast is allowed to break the fast and will have to make it up at a later date. However to break a fast of Ramaḍān without such an excuse would necessitate Kaffārah (to keep sixty consecutive fasts).

It is worth noting here that vomiting due to illness (or a factor which causes nausea which was unintentional) does not break the fast. The fast will break if one re-swallows whatever came up into the mouth. To induce vomit and thereafter to vomit a mouthful will cause the fast to break, however Kaffārah will not be necessary. Vomiting a mouthful means such an amount when cannot be held back without difficulty.

People who are ill and fear that fasting may be harmful or may delay their recovery are allowed to miss the fasts and make them up at a later date. Those who are terminally ill and are apparently not going to recover, and therefore may not be able to make up the missed fasts will be required to give Fidyah. It should be remembered that if such a person did recover and once again became capable of fasting, then they will have to make up for the missed fasts even if they had paid the Fidyah while sick.

As the institution of Ṣalāh is waived for a person who is unconscious for a day or more, so too is the responsibility of fasting waived.

An ill person who elects not to fast and thereafter dies during the illness will not be responsible for those fasts missed during that illness. However, if one regains health, one will be responsible for making up the number of fasts as there were days between regaining health and their death.

In a case where the time between recovery and death is so short that one was unable to make up missed actions, the wali (close, responsible relative) of the deceased will be responsible for paying the fidyah of the missed actions from a third of the deceased's estate, assuming that they had included this to be done in their will. If they hadn't then it can still be given with the consent of all inheriting relatives. (For more details on the issue of wills, please refer to the Fīsabīlillāh book, "Inheritance.")

Note: A pregnant or breast-feeding lady fearing harm upon herself or the child is also allowed to miss the fasts and thereafter make them up at a later date.

Note: A woman experiencing menses or post-natal bleeding is not to fast during bleeding, but is to make up for them later.

Fidyah

A person who is suffering a terminal illness/injury or is so weak through age as to be unable to fast has permission to give Fidyah for each fast he/she misses.

Fidyah is to give food (1.6 kg of wheat or 3.2 kg of dates or barley) or its equivalent in money (this is to be equal to Ṣadaqah al-fiṭr in value) or to feed a person to his/her fill twice in one day. This equals Fidyah for one missed Farḍ Ṣalāh or Ṣawm. It will need to be given for each action missed.

Fidyah does not need to be given immediately, as one may wish to wait to see if one regains the strength/ability to perform the missed obligations. If one is sure that one's end is near then one should allocate and even arrange to distribute the necessary amount as it will then avoid the complications of inheritance. If, however, one recovers enough to perform the missed fasts, then one will be responsible for their performance.

Note: One should bequest in their will that Fidyah be paid from their estate for every missed Ṣalāh and fast that have not been made up during one's lifetime. (This is why it is important to make a record of the missed Ṣalāh and fasts.)

Note: It must be noted that a person cannot use this as a route to escape performing these obligations. If one were to intentionally miss performing the Farḍ acts hoping to give Fidyah instead, will be committing a very severe sin which inherits Allāh's anger and wrath.

Medication During Fasting

Taking any medication orally will render the fast invalid. In the case of necessary medication, only one fast will have to be kept in place of the broken fast, Kaffārah will not be necessary.

Medication not taken orally is divided in two categories. The first is that which provides nutritional benefit for the body (this includes drips and injections which can keep a person alive). This category will break the fast and make Qaḍā' necessary. The second type is that which does not provide nutritional benefit to the body (this includes items such as skin creams, lotions, even nitrates for angina sufferers which can be absorbed by the bloodstream etc). This type is seen by most scholars as not damaging to the fast.

One who suffers from such a condition which requires the daily usage of medication should first consult their doctor to see if medication can be taken outside the times of fasting or if other non-oral alternatives of the medication exist. In this case they may be able to take their medication without breaking their fast.

If medication has to be taken during the day and non-oral alternatives of the medication are not available, then fasting should be delayed and made up after one recovers, It should be noted that not taking prescribed medication or delaying its intake to allow one to fast is not required by the shari'ah and putting one's health at risk in this manner is not sensible.

Unconsciousness During Ramaḍān

If someone was to lose for the whole of Ramaḍān (beginning before the new moon of Ramaḍān is sighted), they will be excused from making up the fasts of that month. However, if at any time during the month of Ramaḍān they were to regain sanity (even for a few moments) they will be responsible for making up all the fasts missed during that month, if they recover. If a person was to lose sanity during Ramaḍān, then the missed fasts, will have to be made up.

If a person was to lose consciousness, whether for the full month or a few days, they will need to keep all missed fasts upon recovery.

Ḥajj

Ḥajj (pilgrimage) is an obligation on every sane, mature Muslim who has the necessary funds to complete the Ḥajj. If due to old age or weakness someone is unable to perform the Ḥajj, but they possess the necessary funds, they may hire someone to fulfil this obligation on their behalf. This is known as Ḥajj Badal.

For Ḥajj Badal to be valid it is necessary that the person being appointed to perform the Ḥajj must already have performed his/her own Farḍ Ḥajj.

In the case that someone has died in a state that the Ḥajj had become necessary on them, then providing that they had made a bequest for it to be performed on their in their will, arrangements will be made to hire someone to do so. This can be a relative/heir. However, the total cost of this cannot be more than a third of the value of the total estate. If it does exceed this amount, then it will only be fulfilled if any of the heirs give consent to their share being decreased by the difference.

For the full procedure of Ḥajj, including; rulings regarding the sick performing Ḥajj; falling ill during Ḥajj; etc, please refer to the Fīsabīlillāh Publication, *Ḥajj: The Journey of a lifetime.*

Islamic View on Medical Treatment

Islām does not discourage medical treatment, but rather encourages it as long as it is done in the knowledge that Allāh ﷻ is truly the one who grants cure to whom He wills, when He wills.

Jābir ؓ narrated that the Prophet of Allāh ﷺ said,
"For every illness there is a cure. Thus, if the cure of the illness is found, (the afflicted one) will be cured by the Will of Allāh." Muslim

Ibn Mas`ūd ؓ reported that the Prophet ﷺ said,
"Allāh did not send down an illness but He sent down a cure with it."
Ibn Ḥibbān

Hilāl ibn Yasāf ﷺ narrated that a man was wounded at the time of the Prophet ﷺ who instructed, "Call a doctor for him."
The companions asked, "Will a doctor benefit him?"
The Prophet replied, 'Yes, for Allāh has not sent down an illness but has sent down a cure." al-Istidhkār

Anas ؓ reported that he heard Rasūlullāh ؓ say,
"Indeed Allāh, where He created illness also created cure, so make use of medication." Muṣannaf ibn Abī Shaybah

The Fiqh of Ḥarām Medication

Medical treatment is permissible as long as it is not using something which is harām.

Umm Salamah ؓ narrates that she heard the Rasūl of Allāh ﷺ say,
"Allāh has not placed cure for you in anything Ḥarām." Ibn Ḥibbān

Although this ḥadīth clearly denoted that cure from illness cannot be attained through something ḥarām, it is often the case that one is presented with medication or treatment which oppose the teachings of Islām. It may be the case that although the actual drug being prescribed is not actually ḥarām, it may be mixed with other ingredients or derived from sources which are ḥarām. For such situations, Muslim jurists have deduced the following laws from the Qur'ān and Sunnah:

1. Usage of ḥarām medication or treatment is only permissible when the medicine or treatment is known to be effective and that there is no other available alternative. Such treatment will only be permissible in cases of Ḍarūrah and Ḥājah, but not for Taḥsīn.

Note:
Ḍarūrah is a situation in which one's life is at risk.

Ḥājah refers to a situation where although one's life is not at risk, there is substantial pain or discomfort.

Therefore, in both of these situations ḥarām medication will be permissible to save one's life or to relieve pain or discomfort.

Taḥsīn refers to beautification and so for cosmetic reasons such medical treatment will not be permitted.

2. Usage of ḥarām treatment due to Ḍarūrah or Ḥājah will be limited to the need; therefore, when the medication or treatment is no longer required it will no longer remain permissible.

The above laws and principles also apply to situations involved within treatment. For example, exposing the satr (private parts) in front of a healthcare professional will be allowed only in times of Ḍarūrah and Ḥājah for as long as it is deemed necessary.

Fiqh of Treatment by the Opposite Sex

Islām strictly forbids unnecessary interaction or seclusion with members of the opposite sex who are not maḥram (i.e. to whom marriage is permitted). But at a time of need, such as medical treatment, some concessions may be applicable.

Treatment by a non-maḥram of the opposite sex is allowed if there is a need and a healthcare professional of the same sex is not available. In such situations, especially if seclusion with the healthcare professional is involved, efforts should be made to have a maḥram (parent, spouse etc) present or to at least have a chaperone (usually available for female patients being treated by a male healthcare professional).

It should be noted that in some situations, such as a hospital setting, where although both male and female healthcare workers will be found, they may not be available at all times due to other commitments or as it would cause disruption to the care of other patients. In such situations receiving treatment by a member of the opposite sex will also be allowed.

Islamic Medical Ethics

It must be noted that many rulings of Sharī`ah discussed hereunder are in regards to contemporary issues; some of which are still under discussion amongst Muslim jurists. Therefore not all rulings listed are unanimously accepted by all jurists.

We advise that in such cases one is not obliged to follow the rulings listed below and thus, one may contact their local scholars and/or other reliable sources for more information and guidance in regards to the following rulings. It should also be remembered that certain issues are such that rulings have to be given upon taking individual cases into consideration and a blanket ruling is almost impossible to give.

Reproduction and Child Birth

Contraception

There are fundamentally two methods of contraception or family planning.

(1) Permanent methods
(2) Temporary methods

It is of utmost importance that one remember that neither method is permissible if adopted for financial reasons, i.e. fear of not being able to financially sustain one's family.

Permanent Methods

Permanent methods include procedures such as vasectomy, tubectomy, castration, sterilisation etc. Scholars unanimously agree that permanent methods of family planning are prohibited since they involve changing human physiology.

Some scholars, however, have allowed procedures such as tubectomy in extreme circumstances; for example, the case of a woman who has been told by medical experts she will be placing her life at risk by conceiving and giving birth to a child. It must be remembered that this is not the norm nor is it applicable if one "just does not want kids", but it is only given as a safety precaution in a desperate situation.

In the Qur'ān Allāh ﷻ quotes the accursed Shaytan,

"'I will mislead them, and I will create in them false desires;
I will order them to slit the ears of cattle,
and to deface the (fair) nature created by Allāh.'
Whoever, forsaking Allāh, takes Shayṭān for a friend,
has surely suffered a loss that is manifest."

Qur'ān an-Nisā 4:119

Temporary Methods

Temporary methods of contraception are permissible according to some scholars if they do not have harmful side effects.

Coitus Interruptus (`Azl)

Coitus interruptus (withdrawal before ejaculation during intercourse) is a temporary form of birth control deemed permissible as long as it is performed with mutual consent of both the husband and wife since both of them have an equal right to have children.

Jābir ؓ, a companion of the Prophet ﷺ, said,
"We used to practice coitus interruptus during the lifetime of Allāh's Messenger, while the Qur'ān was being revealed." al-Bukhāri

Abortion (Medical Termination of Pregnancy)

`Abdullāh ؓ narrated that the Prophet ﷺ said,
"Each of you was put together in the womb of their mother in forty days, then it (the assembled matter) becomes a clot of thick blood for a similar period, then it becomes a piece of flesh for a similar period, then Allāh sends an angel who is ordered to write four things, it is said to him, 'Write his (the child's) deeds, his livelihood, his (time and

manner of) death, and whether he will be blessed or wretched in the Hereafter.' The soul is then breathed into him." al-Bukhārī

From the above tradition of the Prophet, jurists have concluded that the soul, the essence of a human, enters the developing foetus after 120 days of gestation and therefore have ruled abortion thereafter as completely impermissible unless there is a genuine threat to the mother's life.

Even before the period of 120 days, abortion is not permissible; unless performed for a valid reason. Reasons for the abortion should be examined by scholars and medical experts on an individual basis to determine their validity. Valid reasons may include those related to the mother, such a threat to the mother's life, or those reasons related to the child, such as proven abnormalities or genetic diseases which will cause relentless pain to the child and will be an undue burden on the parents and have been proven with certainty to exist in the foetus.

NB: It is not possible to give a list of all valid reasons for abortion before 120 days as they are given after taking personal circumstances into consideration. We therefore advise our readers to contact local reliable scholars and resources in such cases.

Infertility Treatment - Artificial Insemination and Surrogacy

According to all reliable jurists, if any infertility treatment is permitted it would only be artificial insemination using spermatozoa from the husband and the ova and womb of his wife. Any technique in which a third party is involved would strictly be disallowed as this would lead to major complications in identifying the true parents of the child. Therefore, surrogacy, ovum/sperm donation would be deemed impermissible in Islām. The rewarding alternative would be adoption.

Issues Relating to Death

Euthanasia

Islām takes a positive stance against active termination of life. In fact, the Sharī`ah holds such a strong stance against active euthanasia that the Prophet ﷺ strictly forbade even asking death from Allāh ﷻ.

Qais ؓ narrated, "I came to Khabbāb ؓ (a companion of the Prophet ﷺ) who had been branded with seven brands over his abdomen (as a treatment for a severe ailment he was suffering from) and I heard him say, 'If the Prophet had not forbidden us to pray for death, I would have prayed for it."

al-Bukhārī

Anas ؓ narrated that Allāh's Messenger ﷺ said,
"None of you should long for death because of a calamity that has befallen him, and if he cannot but long for death (due to the severity of the condition) then they should say,

اَللّٰهُمَّ أَحْيِنِيْ مَا كَانَتِ الْحَيَاةُ خَيْرًا لِّيْ
وَتَوَفَّنِيْ مَا كَانَتِ الْوَفَاةُ خَيْرًا لِّيْ

ALLĀHUMMA 'AḤYINĪ MĀ KĀNATIL ḤAYĀTU KHAYRAL-LĪ, WA TAWAFFANĪ 'IDHĀ KĀNATIL WAFĀTU KHAYRAL-LĪ.

'O Allāh, let me live as long as long as life is better for me, and take my life if death is better for me.'"

al-Bukhārī

Islamic beliefs sternly dictate that Allah ﷻ is solely responsible for deciding when someone's life is to end and therefore any human intervention in actively ending someone's life would be considered a erious offence unless deemed lawful in an Islamic court of law (e.g. omeone sentenced to capital punishment).

The question arises as to what guidance Islām offers regarding passive euthanasia, where death is brought about not due to active intervention but rather due to withholding or withdrawing treatment equired to maintain human life. Here, Muslim jurists have ruled that where an available treatment is seen as certainly curing the ailment and prolonging life (as proven by thorough medical research), withholding or withdrawing such treatment would be deemed as impermissible. On the other hand, where there is no reliable evidence reliable in the medical field) and so medical treatment may or may not be of benefit, then withdrawing, withholding or even the patient rejecting treatment themselves would be seen as permissible and so death thereafter would not be seen as euthanasia or suicide.

Brain Stem Death and the Permanent Vegetative State

The brain stem is the area of the brain responsible for controlling vital functions such as respiration and swallowing. The loss of this area of the brain, once confirmed by medical professionals, will confirm the passing away of an individual, although certain processes may continue due to the support of machines (for example, the heart may continue to beat if the individual is placed on life support although tests may confirm brain stem death). In such cases, the individual will be considered deceased by Muslim jurist and so life support and other treatment should be stopped.

In contrast, the permanent vegetative state is where an individual is in a coma, with no hope of recovery due to irreversible damage to the brain, but is breathing on their own without the aid of a ventilator. An individual in such a state may live for years providing they are fed and taken care of. Islām decrees that in such a state, as it is certain feeding is required to keep such an individual alive, it will therefore be necessary to continue feeding and caring for such patients. Their physical or mental state will not permit feeding to be stopped.

Some, deficient of faith in the Hereafter, may argue that keeping such an individual alive is not only pointless but a waste of money and resources as there is no hope of recovery; however, we find in the teaching of the Messenger ﷺ that such an individual may be gaining a great deal, as Allāh ﷻ prepares them for eternal bliss by cleansing them of their sins in this world.

`Abdur-Raḥmān ibn Azhar ؓ narrated that the Prophet ﷺ said,
"The example of a believing servant when illness or fever afflicts him is of iron entering fire, its scum leaves and its goodness remains." al-Ḥākim

Rasūlullāh ﷺ was reported to have said,
"The state of a believer and his unease with illness is amazing. If he were to know what (reward) was for him in illness he would wish to be ill forever."
aṭ-Ṭabarānī

Therefore, what apparently seems to be pain and discomfort preceding death may in reality be a great blessing in disguise, as Allāh ﷻ prepares His chosen servants for eternal happiness in the Hereafter by giving them a minor form of discomfort in this life, thus relieving them of the greater pain and discomfort of the Hereafter.

Organ and Tissue Transplantation

The issue of organ transplantation has been extensively discussed by Muslim jurists resulting in opposing opinions.

According to many scholars, organ and tissue transplantation from a living donor is allowed when necessary provided the donor's consent is taken, and they are not placed in any significant danger, as one life cannot be sacrificed to save another. Therefore blood transfusions and bone marrow transplants would be considered permissible as the donor is not put at any major risk.

"...and if any one saved a life, it would be as if he saved the life of the whole people."

Qur'ān, al-Mā'idah, 5:32

In relation to transplanting materials from the dead, some scholars permit it as long as the deceased's consent was given prior to their death and their sanctity is maintained in removing the organs or other material. This is because the Prophet of Allāh ﷺ strictly forbade mutilating a dead body.

`Imrān ibn Ḥuṣayn ؓ narrated, "The Prophet did not deliver to us a sermon but (in each one of them he) ordered us give charity and forbade us from mutilating (the human body)." al-Ḥākim

Other scholars insist that permission can only be granted if the deceased's relatives also consent to the removal of organs.

The scholars permitting organ transplantation have also ruled organ donation permissible, therefore permitting Muslims to carry donor cards. It is worth noting organ donation is allowed, but the sale of organs or any other part of a human is strictly forbidden in Islam. Therefore, to even take a payment for giving blood would be classed as earning unlawfully.

One must however, remember that this is not the view of all, and so a person should take the views of their local scholars.

Supplications

As discussed earlier, Allāh ﷾ alone is truly the One Who cures illness and therefore in sickness and in health we should do our utmost to pray to Him. During illness we should pray and ask that He cures us, and in health we should ask Him to maintain our health and save us from illness.

Although illness may be a cause of severe distress or pain, it is a time when one should pay particular attention to all acts of worship, especially the obligatory prayers. It is Allāh ﷾ Who grants cure and therefore it would be highly arrogant that whilst in the hope that Allāh ﷾ grants us cure, we disobey Him. One is free to take advantage of the concessions that may apply to them during their illness but they shouldn't allow their illness to become an excuse to flout the Laws of their Lord ﷾.

After obligatory prayer, one should engage in the various forms of Dhikr (remembrance of Allāh ﷾) and prayers. Time should be specially allocated for this, rather than considering it as a might-as-well entity.

Allāh ﷾ states,

"O you who believe, celebrate the praises of Allāh, and do so often; and glorify Him morning and evening."

Qur'ān, al-Aḥzāb, 33:41-42

The remembrance of Allāh ﷾ is also a source of piece and tranquillity.

"Those who believe, and whose hearts find satisfaction in the remembrance of Allāh: for without doubt in the remembrance of Allāh do hearts find satisfaction."

Qur'ān, ar-Ra`d, 13:28

It is advised that one also spends time reciting the Qur'ān, as it too is a source of Shifā (cure), as well as it being the best form of Dhikr.

Allāh ﷻ states,

"We send down (stage by stage) in the Qur'ān that which is a healing and a mercy to those who believe: to the unjust it causes nothing but loss after loss."

Qur'ān, al-Isrā, 17:82

Additionally one may allocate time to other forms of prayer including supplicating to Allāh ﷻ. Du`ā' can be described as a servant's direct conversation with their Master in which they may ask for whatever their heart desires, providing they are not asking for something unlawful. This can be done in any state, at any time, in any language.

Anas ؓ reported that the Messenger of Allāh ﷺ said,
"Du`ā' (supplication) is the essence of worship." at-Tirmidhī

Included now are some examples of supplications made by the Messenger of Allāh ﷺ, or his companions ؓ for such occasions.

SUPPLICATIONS

At the Time of Pain

`Uthmān ibn Abī al-`Āṣ ☙ reported that he complained to the Prophet of Allāh ﷺ about a pain he had in his body, so the Messenger of Allāh ﷺ replied, "Place your hand on the area you feel the pain and say three times:

بِسْمِ اللهِ

BISMIL-LĀH

In the name of Allāh

and then read seven times:

أَعُوذُ بِاللهِ وَقُدْرَتِهِ مِنْ شَرِّ مَا أَجِدُ وَأُحَاذِرُ

'A`ŪDHU BIL-LĀHI WA QUDRATIHĪ
MIN SHARRI MĀ 'AJIDU WA 'UḤĀDHIR.

I seek refuge in Allāh and in His power
from the evil that afflicts me and that which I apprehend."

Muslim

Prayers to Recite When Visiting the Sick

`Ā'ishah ☙ narrated that the Prophet ﷺ, when he visited an ill person or when an ill person was brought to him, would say,

أَذْهِبِ الْبَأْسَ رَبَ النَّاسِ اشْفِ وَأَنْتَ الشَّافِي

لَا شِفَاءَ إِلَّا شِفَاؤُكَ شِفَاءً لَّا يُغَادِرُ سَقَمًا

'ADH-HIBIL BA'SA RABBUN-NĀS,
'ISHFI WA 'ANTASH-SHĀFĪ,
LĀ SHIFĀ'A 'ILLĀ SHIFĀ'UK,
SHIFĀ'UL-LĀ YUGHĀDIRU SAQAMĀ.

"Remove the agony, O Lord of Man.
Cure (him/her): You are the (true) Giver of cure,
there is no cure but Your cure,
(which is) such a cure which leaves behind no disease."

al-Bukhārī

`Abdullāh ibn `Abbās ﷺ narrates, "Whenever the Prophet ﷺ would visit any sick person he would say,

لَا بَأْسَ طَهُوْرٌ إِنْ شَاءَ اللهُ

LĀ BA'SA ṬAHŪRUN, IN SHĀ'AL-LĀH.

"It (the sickness) is no problem, but (it is) a cure,
If Allāh so wills."

al-Bukhārī

`Alī ﷺ narrates, "The Prophet visited me when I was ill, at which time I was praying, 'O Allāh! if my time (of death) has come, have mercy on me; and if my time is later, raise me; and if it is a test, make me patient.'

"He (The Prophet) asked, 'What did you say?'

"I repeated what I had prayed. On this the Prophet said,

اَللّٰهُمَّ اشْفِهِ اَللّٰهُمَّ عَافِهِ

ALLĀHUM-MASH-FIHĪ, ALLĀHUMMA `ĀFIHĪ

'O Allāh! Cure him. O Allāh! relieve him.'

"He then told me to stand, and I stood. I never suffered from that illness after that."

al-Ḥākim

`Abdullāh ibn `Abbās ⸙ narrates from the Prophet ﷺ, "If a Muslim servant (of Allāh ﷻ) visits an infirm, whose time (of death) has not come, and reads seven times (the following supplication), he (the infirm) will be relieved of his difficulty."

أَسْأَلُ اللهَ الْعَظِيْمَ رَبَّ الْعَرْشِ الْعَظِيْمِ أَنْ يَّشْفِيَكَ

'AS'ALUL-LĀHAL `AẒĪMA RABBAL `ARSHIL `AẒĪMI 'AY-YASHFIYAK.

I ask Almighty Allāh, Lord of the great Throne, to make you well.

at-Tirmidhī and Abū Dāwūd

Prayers to Recite if Terminally/Seriously Ill

اَللّٰهُمَّ اغْفِرْ لِيْ وَارْحَمْنِيْ وَأَلْحِقْنِيْ بِالرَّفِيْقِ الْأَعْلٰى

'ALLĀHUM-MAGHFIR LĪ WAR-ḤAMNĪ WA 'ALḤIQNĪ BIR-RAFĪQIL 'A`LĀ.

O Allāh, forgive me and have mercy upon me
and join me with the highest companion (in Paradise).

al-Bukhārī and Muslim

Examples of the Prophets' عليه السلام Supplications in the Qur'ān

The following two prayers were made by the Prophets Ayyūb عليه السلام and Nūḥ عليه السلام respectively, both at times of incredible suffering and pain, which were caused either by illness or testing. The words of these simple yet powerful entreaties convey their unwavering faith in the Lord سبحانه وتعالى, even in the face of the most formidable challenges.

إِنِّي مَسَّنِيَ الضُّرُّ وَأَنتَ أَرْحَمُ الرَّاحِمِينَ ﴿٨٣﴾

‘ANNĪ MASSANIYAḌ-ḌURRU
WA ‘ANTA ‘ARḤAMUR-RĀḤIMĪN.

Truly distress has seized me, But You are the most Merciful One.

Qur'ān, al-Ambiya, 21:83

إِنِّي مَغْلُوبٌ فَانتَصِرْ ﴿١٠﴾

‘ANNĪ MAGHLŪBUN FAN-TAṢIR

I am one overcome: so help (me).

Qur'ān, al-Qamar, 54:10

In the Qur'ān, they are mentioned as parts of complete sentences, and so are pre-fixed with أَنِّي ('annī); for the purpose of using them separately as Du`ā' this shall be replaced with إِنِّي ('innī).

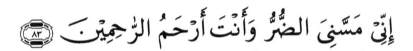

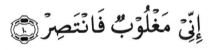

Prayers from the Qur'ān for General Purposes

رَبَّنَآ ءَاتِنَا فِي الدُّنْيَا حَسَنَةً وَفِي الْآخِرَةِ حَسَنَةً
وَقِنَا عَذَابَ النَّارِ ﴿٢٠١﴾

**RABBANĀ 'ĀTINĀ FID-DUNYĀ ḤASANAH,
WA FIL 'ĀKHIRATI ḤASANAH,
WA QINĀ `ADHĀBAN-NĀR.**

**Our Lord! Give us good in this world and good in the Hereafter,
and defend us from the torment of the Fire!**

Qur'ān, al-Baqarah, 2:201

رَبَّنَا وَلَا تُحَمِّلْنَا مَا لَا طَاقَةَ لَنَا بِهِۦ
وَاعْفُ عَنَّا وَاغْفِرْ لَنَا وَارْحَمْنَآ ۚ أَنتَ مَوْلَىٰنَا
فَانصُرْنَا عَلَى الْقَوْمِ الْكَٰفِرِينَ ﴿٢٨٦﴾

**RABBANĀ WA LĀ TUḤAMMILNĀ
MĀ LĀ ṬĀQATA LANĀ BIH.
WA`FU `ANNĀ, WAGH-FIRLANĀ,
WAR-ḤAMNĀ, 'ANTA MAWLĀNĀ
FAN-ṢURNĀ `ALAL QAWMIL KĀFIRĪN.**

**Our Lord! lay not on us a burden
greater than we have strength to bear.
Blot out our sins, and grant us forgiveness.
Have mercy on us. You are our Protector;
so help us against those who are unfaithful (to You).**

Qur'ān, al-Baqarah, 2:286

فَاطِرَ السَّمٰوٰتِ وَالْأَرْضِ أَنْتَ وَلِيّٖ فِي الدُّنْيَا وَالْاٰخِرَةِ ۚ
تَوَفَّنِيْ مُسْلِمًا وَّأَلْحِقْنِيْ بِالصّٰلِحِيْنَ ﴿١٠١﴾

FĀṬIRAS-SAMĀWĀTI WAL 'ARḌ,
'ANTA WALIYYĪ FID-DUNYĀ WAL 'ĀKHIRAH.
TAWAFFANĪ MUSLIMAW-WA 'ALḤIQNĪ BIṢ-ṢĀLIḤĪN.

(O) Creator of the heavens and the earth!
You are my Protector in this world and in the Hereafter.
Take my soul (at death) as a Muslim,
and unite me with the righteous.

Qur'ān, Yūsuf, 12:101

قُلْ أَعُوْذُ بِرَبِّ الْفَلَقِ ﴿١﴾
مِنْ شَرِّ مَا خَلَقَ ﴿٢﴾
وَمِنْ شَرِّ غَاسِقٍ إِذَا وَقَبَ ﴿٣﴾
وَمِنْ شَرِّ النَّفّٰثٰتِ فِي الْعُقَدِ ﴿٤﴾
وَمِنْ شَرِّ حَاسِدٍ إِذَا حَسَدَ ﴿٥﴾

QUL 'A`ŪDHU BI RABBIL FALAQ.
MIN SHARRI MĀ KHALAQ.
WA MIN SHARRI GHĀSIQIN 'IDHĀ WAQAB.
WA MIN SHARRIN-NAF-FĀTHĀTI FIL `UQAD.
WA MIN SHARRI ḤĀSIDIN 'IDHĀ ḤASAD.

Say: I seek refuge with the Lord of the Dawn,
From the mischief of created things;
From the mischief of Darkness as it overspreads;
From the mischief of those who blow on knots
(practice witchcraft);
And from the mischief of the envious one as he practices envy.

Qur'ān, al-Falaq, 113

قُلْ أَعُوذُ بِرَبِّ النَّاسِ ﴿١﴾ مَلِكِ النَّاسِ ﴿٢﴾

إِلَٰهِ النَّاسِ ﴿٣﴾ مِن شَرِّ الْوَسْوَاسِ الْخَنَّاسِ ﴿٤﴾

الَّذِي يُوَسْوِسُ فِي صُدُورِ النَّاسِ ﴿٥﴾

مِنَ الْجِنَّةِ وَالنَّاسِ ﴿٦﴾

QUL 'A`ŪDHU BI RABBIN-NĀS.
MALIKIN-NĀS. 'ILĀHIN-NĀS.
MIN SHARRIL WASWĀSIL KHANNĀS.
'ALLADHĪ YUWASWISU FĪ SUDŪRIN-NĀS.
MINAL JINNATI WAN-NĀS.

Say: I seek refuge with the Lord of Mankind,
The Ruler over Mankind, The God of Mankind,
From the evil of the whisperer, who (afterwards) withdraws,
Who whispers into the hearts of Mankind,
(Who are from) amongst the Jinns and Men.

Qur'ān, an-Nās, 114

Prayers from the Aḥādīth for General Purposes

Abū Umāmah ﵁ narrates that the Messenger of Allāh ﷺ made many different supplications which we found difficult to memorise, so we mentioned this (problem) to him, to which he replied,
'Shall I not show you a du`ā' which includes all of that (which I have asked). Say...

اَللّٰهُمَّ إِنَّا نَسْأَلُكَ مِنْ خَيْرِ مَا سَأَلَكَ مِنْهُ نَبِيُّكَ مُحَمَّدٌ

وَنَعُوْذُ بِكَ مِنْ شَرِّ مَا اسْتَعَاذَ مِنْهُ نَبِيُّكَ مُحَمَّدٌ

وَأَنْتَ الْمُسْتَعَانُ وَعَلَيْكَ الْبَلَاغُ

وَلَا حَوْلَ وَلَا قُوَّةَ إِلَّا بِاللهِ

**'ALLĀHUMMA 'INNĀ NAS'ALUKA MIN KHAYRI
MĀ SA'ALAKA MINHU NABIY-YUKA MUḤAMMAD,
WA NA`ŪDHU BIKA MIN SHARRI MAS-TA`ĀDHA
MINHU NABIY-YUKA MUḤAMMAD,
WA 'ANTAL MUSTA`ĀN, WA `ALAYKAL BALĀGH,
WA LĀ ḤAWLA WA LĀ QUWWATA 'IL-LĀ BILLĀH.**

O Allāh! we ask for the good Your Prophet Muḥammad asked for;
and we seek protection from the evil
Your Prophet Muḥammad sought protection from.
Verily from You is help sought, and upon You is deliverance.
There is no power nor might apart from what is Yours.

at-Tirmidhī

اَللّٰهُمَّ احْرُسْنِي بِعَيْنِكَ الَّتِيْ لَا تَنَامُ

وَاكْنُفْنِي بِرُكْنِكَ الَّذِيْ لَا يُرَامُ

وَارْحَمْنِي بِقُدْرَتِكَ عَلَيَّ لَا أَهْلِكُ وَأَنْتَ رَجَائِيْ

فَكَمْ مِّنْ نِعْمَةٍ أَنْعَمْتَ بِهَا عَلَيَّ قَلَّ لَكَ عِنْدَهَا شُكْرِيْ

وَكَمْ مِّنْ بَلِيَّةٍ اِبْتَلَيْتَنِيْ قَلَّ لَكَ بِهَا صَبْرِيْ

فَيَا مَنْ قَلَّ عِنْدَ نِعْمَتِهٖ شُكْرِيْ فَلَمْ تَحْرُمْنِيْ

وَيَا مَنْ قَلَّ عِنْدَ بَلِيَّتِهٖ صَبْرِيْ فَلَمْ تَخْذُلْنِيْ

وَيَا مَنْ رَّاٰنِيْ عَلَى الْخَطَايَا فَلَمْ تَفْضَحْنِيْ

أَسْأَلُكَ أَنْ تُصَلِّيَ عَلٰى مُحَمَّدٍ وَّعَلٰى اٰلِ مُحَمَّدٍ كَمَا صَلَّيْتَ

وَبَارَكْتَ وَرَحِمْتَ عَلٰى إِبْرَاهِيْمَ إِنَّكَ حَمِيْدٌ مَّجِيْدٌ

اَللّٰهُمَّ أَعِنِّيْ عَلٰى دِيْنِيْ بِدُنْيَا وَعَلٰى اٰخِرَتِيْ بِتَقْوٰى

وَاحْفَظْنِيْ فِيْمَا غِبْتُ عَنْهُ وَلَا تَكِلْنِيْ إِلٰى نَفْسِيْ فِيْمَا حَضَرْتُ

‘ALLĀHUM-MAḤRUSNĪ BI `AYNIKAL-LATĪ LĀ TANĀM,
WAK-NUFNĪ BI RUKNIKAL-LADHĪ LĀ YURĀM,
WAR-ḤAMNĪ BI QUDRATIKA `ALAYYA LĀ ‘AHLIKU,
WA ‘ANTA RĀJĀ’Ī, FA
KAM MIN NI`MATIN ‘AN`AMTA BIHĀ `ALAYYA
QALLA LAKA `INDAHĀ SHUKRĪ,
WA KAM MIN BALIYYATI-NIBTALAYTANĪ
QALLA LAKA BIHĀ ṢABRĪ,
FA YĀ MAN QALLA `INDA NI`MATIHĪ SHUKRĪ
FA LAM TAḤRIMNĪ,
WA YĀ MAN QALLA `INDA BALIYYATIHĪ ṢABRĪ
FA LAM TAKH-DHULNĪ,
WA YĀ MAR-RA'ĀNĪ `ALAL-KHAṬĀYĀ
FA LAM TAFḌAHNĪ,
‘AS’ALUKA ‘AN TUṢAL-LĪYA `ALĀ MUḤAMMAD,
WA `ALĀ ‘ĀLI MUḤAMMAD KAMĀ ṢALLAYTA
WA BĀRAKTA WA RAḤIMTA `ALĀ ‘IBRĀHĪM,
‘IN-NAKA ḤAMĪDUM-MAJĪD.
ALLĀHUMMA ‘A`IN-NĪ `ALĀ DĪNĪ BI DUNYĀ,
WA `ALĀ ‘ĀKHIRATĪ BI TAQWĀ,
WAḤ-FAẒNĪ FĪMĀ GHIBTU `ANHU,
WA LĀ TAKILNĪ ‘ILĀ NAFSĪ FĪMĀ ḤAḌARTU

O Allāh guard me with Your eye that does not sleep.
And shroud me with Your support that does not leave exposed,
and have mercy on me with Your strength over me
so I do not perish. You are my hope.
How many blessings are there that You have bestowed upon me,
and my appreciation is deficient,
and how many problems there are with which You have tested me
and my patience was deficient.
O He for Whose blessings my gratitude was scant,
but still did not deprive me.
O He, Who tested me with problems for which my patience
was scant but did not forsake me.

O He, Who saw me sinning but did not disgrace me.
I ask You to shower You mercy upon Muḥammad
and the family of Muḥammad,
as how You showered Your mercy, blessings and mercy on Ibrāhīm.
Indeed You are the praiseworthy, glorious.
O Allāh! help me in my religion through the world
and help me with the hereafter through Taqwā (God-conciousness).
And protect me from what I was absent from (i.e. what is hidden from me), and do not entrust me to myself in what befalls me.

Tārīkh Madīnah ad-Dimishk

أَسْأَلُكَ الْعَافِيَةَ مِنْ كُلِّ بَلِيَّةٍ وَأَسْأَلُكَ الشُّكْرَ عَلَى الْعَافِيَةِ
وَأَسْأَلُكَ دَوَامَ الْعَافِيَةِ وَأَسْأَلُكَ الْغِنٰى عَنِ النَّاسِ
وَلَا حَوْلَ وَلَا قُوَّةَ إِلَّا بِاللهِ الْعَلِيِّ الْعَظِيْمِ

'AS'ALUKAL `ĀFIYATA MIN KULLI BALIYYAH,
WA 'AS'ALUKASH-SHUKRA `ALAL `ĀFIYAH,
WA 'AS'ALUKA DAWĀMAL `ĀFIYAH,
WA 'AS'ALUKAL GINĀ `ANIN-NĀS.
WA LĀ ḤAWLĀ WA LĀ QUWWATA
'ILLĀ BIL-LĀHIL `ALIYYIL `AẒĪM.

I ask You for well-being from all afflictions, and I ask You (to make me) grateful on the well-being, and I ask You for unending well-being, and I ask You for freedom/independance from people.
There is no power and no strength but in Allāh,
the exalted, the Great.

Musnad al-Firdaws

اَللّٰهُمَّ اهْدِنَا فِيمَنْ هَدَيْتَ وَعَافِنَا فِيمَنْ عَافَيْتَ

وَتَوَلَّنَا فِيمَنْ تَوَلَّيْتَ وَبَارِكْ لَنَا فِيمَا أَعْطَيْتَ

وَقِنَا شَرَّ مَا قَضَيْتَ إِنَّكَ تَقْضِي وَلَا يُقْضٰى عَلَيْكَ

إِنَّهٗ لَا يَذِلُّ مَنْ وَّالَيْتَ تَبَارَكْتَ وَتَعَالَيْتَ

'ALLĀHUM-MAHDINĀ FĪ MAN HADAYT,
WA `ĀFINĀ FĪ MAN `ĀFAYT,
WA TAWAL-LANĀ FĪ MAN TAWAL-LAYT,
WA BĀRIK LANĀ FĪ MĀ 'A`ṬAYT,
WA QINĀ SHARRA MĀ QAḌAYT.
'INNAKA TAQḌĪ WA LĀ YUQḌĀ `ALAYK,
'INNAHŪ LĀ YADHILLU MAW-WĀLAYT,
TABĀRAKTA WA TA`ĀLAYT.

O Allāh guide us with those whom You have guided.
And grant us ease with those whom You have granted ease.
And befriend us with those whom You have befriended.
And give us blessing in what You have given us.
And protect us from the evil which You have ordained.
Verily You decree and You are not decreed over.
Verily he who You befriend will not be humiliated.
You are praised and You are supreme.

Ibn Ḥibbān and al-Ḥākim

اَللّٰهُمَّ اقْسِمْ لَنَا مِنْ خَشْيَتِكَ مَا يَحُوْلُ بَيْنَنَا وَبَيْنَ مَعَاصِيكَ

وَمِنْ طَاعَتِكَ مَا تُبَلِّغُنَا بِهٖ جَنَّتَكَ

وَمِنَ الْيَقِيْنِ مَا تُهَوِّنُ بِهِ عَلَيْنَا مُصِيْبَاتِ الدُّنْيَا

وَمَتِّعْنَا بِأَسْمَاعِنَا وَأَبْصَارِنَا وَقُوَّتِنَا مَا أَحْيَيْتَنَا

وَاجْعَلْهُ الْوَارِثَ مِنَّا وَاجْعَلْ ثَأْرَنَا عَلٰى مَنْ ظَلَمَنَا

وَانْصُرْنَا عَلٰى مَنْ عَادَانَا وَلَا تَجْعَلْ مُصِيْبَتَنَا فِيْ دِيْنِنَا

وَلَا تَجْعَلِ الدُّنْيَا أَكْبَرَ هَمِّنَا وَلَا مَبْلَغَ عِلْمِنَا

وَلَا تُسَلِّطْ عَلَيْنَا مَنْ لَّا يَرْحَمُنَا

'ALLĀHUM-MAQSIM LANĀ MIN KHASH-YATIKA
MĀ YAḤŪLU BAYNANĀ WA BAYNA MA`ĀṢĪK,
WA MIN ṬĀ`ATIKA MĀ TUBAL-LIGHUNĀ BIHĪ JANNATAK,
WA MINAL-YAQĪNI MĀ TUHAW-WINU
BIHĪ `ALAYNĀ MUṢĪBĀTID-DUNYĀ,
WA MATTI`NĀ BI 'ASMĀ`INĀ WA 'ABṢĀRINĀ,
WA QUW-WATINĀ MĀ 'AḤYAYTANĀ,
WAJ`ALHUL WĀRITHA MINNĀ,
WAJ`AL THĀ'RANĀ `ALĀ MAN ẒALAMANĀ,
WAN-ṢURNĀ `ALĀ MAN `ĀDĀNĀ,
WA LĀ TAJ`AL MUṢĪBATANĀ FĪ DĪNINĀ,
WA LĀ TAJ`ALID-DUNYĀ 'AKBARA HAM-MINĀ,
WA LĀ MABLAGHA `ILMINĀ,
WA LĀ TUSAL-LIṬ `ALAYNĀ MAL-LĀ YARḤAMUNĀ.

O Allāh! allot for us (a portion) from Your fear which becomes a barrier between us and Your disobedience, and from Your obedience that which will take us to Your heaven, and from such conviction which makes easy the trials of the world.

Maintain us with (the longevity of) our hearing,
our sight and our strength throughout our lives.
And make it (these portions) an heir from (i.e. forerunning) us,
and avenge us on those who oppress us,
and help us against those that hold us in enmity,
and do not make our trials in our religion,
and do not make the world our greatest goal,
nor the culmination of our knowledge,
and do not set upon us a ruler who does not have mercy on us.

at-Tirmidhī

اَللّٰهُمَّ لَا تَدَعْ لَنَا ذَنْبًا إِلَّا غَفَرْتَهُ

وَلَا هَمًّا إِلَّا فَرَّجْتَهُ وَلَا دَيْنًا إِلَّا قَضَيْتَهُ

وَلَا حَاجَةً مِّنْ حَوَائِجِ الدُّنْيَا وَالْآخِرَةِ

إِلَّا قَضَيْتَهَا بِرَحْمَتِكَ يَا أَرْحَمَ الرَّاحِمِيْنَ

'ALLĀHUMMA LĀ TADA` LANĀ DHAMBAN
'ILLĀ GHAFARTAH,
WA LĀ HAMMAN 'ILLĀ FAR-RAJTAH,
WA LĀ DAYNAN 'ILLĀ QAḌAYTAH,
WA LĀ ḤĀJATAM-MIN ḤAWĀ'IJID-DUNYĀ
WAL 'ĀKHIRAH 'ILLĀ QAḌAYTAHĀ
BI RAḤMATIKA YĀ 'ARḤAMAR-RĀḤIMĪN

O Allāh! leave for us no sin except that You forgive it, and no anxiety except that You relieve it, and no debt except that You fulfill it, and no need from the needs of the world and the hereafter except that You have fulfilled it with Your Mercy, O Most Merciful.

aṭ-Ṭabarānī

CPSIA information can be obtained
at www.ICGtesting.com
Printed in the USA
LVOW13s1918090317
526681LV00012B/1142/P

9 781536 821208